RICHARD ROSENBLUM
MY BAR MITZVAH

William Morrow and Company • New York

Library of Congress Cataloging in Publication Data
Rosenblum, Richard.   My bar mitzvah.   Summary: The author describes the celebration of his bar mitzvah.
1. Bar mitzvah—Juvenile literature. [1. Bar mitzvah]
I. Title. BM707.R63   1985   296.4′424   84-16685
ISBN 0-688-04143-4   ISBN 0-688-04144-2 (lib. bdg.)

To my parents, Anna and Archie

When I was a boy, my family had a secret berry patch. It was in the Catskill Mountains, where we spent every summer.

We picked buckets of huckleberries . . . gallons . . . barrels full. My father worked all week in New York City and visited us on weekends. On Sunday night he took the berry crop home with him. It was for Grandma to make wine for my bar mitzvah.

In the dark corners of the basement of our house in Brooklyn were huge, old clay crocks filled with berries. They were covered with cheesecloth, and they gave off a strange, sweet smell. It was our huckleberries being made into wine.

The basement was a club room for me, my cousins, and our friends. All of my friends lived on my block. I knew everyone who lived in every house.

Our house was brick, with a brick porch in front and a garden in back. My family lived upstairs. Aunt Ruth and Uncle Jack and my cousins, Larry and Renee, lived downstairs.

My cousin Renee took elocution lessons. A lady came to
our house and taught Renee to recite poems using lots of hand
motions. My friends and I made faces outside the window
until my aunt chased us away.

My whole gang went to Hebrew school: Marty, his cousin Arwin, Jackie, Morty—we called him "Goondreckle"—and "Bottlebreaker" Bernstein. None of us liked to go to another class after regular school every day, so we got into as much trouble as possible. Our mothers were called in, but everybody's mother blamed the other boys.

Somehow I learned to read and write Hebrew and to prepare for my bar mitzvah. Bar mitzvah means "son of the commandment." At thirteen, every Jewish boy is expected to understand and be guided by Jewish religious law that has been handed down for thousands of years.

My thirteenth birthday was coming closer.

At home, my mother and Grandma cooked and baked for weeks. They roasted turkeys and chickens and made a fragrant ocean of chicken soup. They made pots of gefilte fish and two kinds of horseradish. They bought herrings by the barrelful and pickled them three different ways. The iceboxes in our house and my aunt's house and our neighbors' houses were all packed with food.

For the big day, my father made me a new suit with a vest and my first pair of long pants. I went to his "shop," the big clothing factory where he worked as a tailor, to try it on.

Everyone was invited to my bar mitzvah. Everyone: my fourteen aunts and uncles and their families and the families of their families; my father's friends from the shop and the union he belonged to; all of our neighbors, which meant the whole block.

The synagogue was filled. My friends from the block sat in the second row and made crazy faces as I read from the Torah scroll. I'd get even at their bar mitzvahs, just as some of them were already getting even with me.

After I delivered my bar mitzvah speech, the rabbi shook my hand, presented me with a Bible, and told the congregation what a wonderful student I was.

Almost the whole congregation marched back to our house.
My mother and Grandma had gone ahead to put the finishing
touches on the feast.

The hungry guests poured in
and were seated. The banquet was
about to begin. Long tables, rented
for the day, were covered with
bottles of seltzer and syrup to make
drinks, bowls of pickled vegetables,
salads, plain and seeded rolls, rye
breads two feet long, and black
breads as round as platters. There
were honey cakes and sponge
cakes. A special bar mitzvah cake
grew in white layers and was
topped with a plaster bar mitzvah
boy.

My great-uncle recited a blessing
over the challah, the Sabbath bread.

Everybody yelled, "Mazel tov,"
which means good luck, and the
meal began.

All day, Uncle Sol was in the kitchen carving turkeys and slicing meat. My mother put a big apron over her dress and pinned her corsage to the apron.

People arrived and left all afternoon and evening. My father handed out cigars and was very happy. He beamed.

Someone gathered my cousins Marilyn, Renee, and
Debbie, my sister Debbie, little Richard (I was big Richard),
Gilbert, my other cousin Renee, Juney, Bunny, Irwin, and
Doris. Cousin Bob took a picture of us. I stood in the middle
with a big smirk on my face.

My father introduced me to his friends from the shop and the union.
I shook hands, and each one handed me a white envelope. When no one
was looking, I gave the envelopes to my father.

After the meal, people sat around in my aunt and uncle's house downstairs. The rooms were filled with happy, laughing guests. They spilled out onto the front porch and into the alley and backyard.

Opening my presents was the best part of the day. I was given a Boy Scout knife with scissors, a bottle-opener, a screwdriver, and a big and little blade. Another gift was a pair of boots that laced up to my knees and had a special pocket on the side for my knife. Admiral Byrd, who went to the South Pole, had a pair just like them.

I got a leather aviator's helmet with real goggles, a three-battery flashlight that you could shine against the clouds at night, and an American flag with a gold fringe and its own collapsible flagpole.

My Aunt Ethel opened a five-dollar savings
account for me. She also wrote to Uncle Don, who
had a show for kids on the radio, and he announced
to the world that today was my bar mitzvah. He also
told me I had a model airplane kit hidden underneath
the record player in the basement.

My parents' aunts and uncles were very old and had come a great distance by subway, bus, and trolley car. The oldest uncle proposed a toast with our huckleberry wine to the bar mitzvah boy. Everyone raised their glasses. I blushed.

Sometime during the evening my cousin Doris tap-danced,
Renee recited poems, and my sister Debbie sang, even though
she couldn't carry a tune. I wasn't there. I was running free
with my gang, trying to aim a searchlight beam on the clouds.

I never did get to open the white envelopes. My parents said the money inside helped them pay for my bar mitzvah.

That was good enough.